RO SPORTS
UPERSTARS

SUPERSTARS OF THE CHICAGO BEARS

by M.K. Osborne

AMICUS | AMICUS INK

Library of Congress Cataloging-in-Publication Data
Names: Osborne, M. K., author.
Title: Superstars of the Chicago Bears / By M.K. Osborne.
Description: Mankato, MN : Amicus, [2019] |
Series: Pro sports superstars NFL | Audience: K to grade 3.| Includes bibliographical references and index.
Identifiers: LCCN 2017057177 (print) | LCCN 2018006975 (ebook) | ISBN 9781681514840 (pdf) | ISBN 9781681514024 (library binding) | ISBN 9781681523224 (pbk.)
Subjects: LCSH: Chicago Bears (Football team)--Biography--Juvenile literature. | Chicago Bears (Football team)--History--Juvenile literature. | Football players--United States--Biography--Juvenile literature.
Classification: LCC GV956.C5 (ebook) | LCC GV956.C5 O83 2019 (print) | DDC 796.332/640977311--dc23 LC record available at https://lccn.loc.gov/2017057177

Photo Credits: All photos from Associated Press except Getty Images/Focus on Sport, 10–11

Series Designer: Veronica Scott
Book Designer: Ciara Beitlich/Veronica Scott
Photo Researcher: Holly Young

Printed in China
HC 10 9 8 7 6 5 4 3 2 1
PB 10 9 8 7 6 5 4 3 2 1

TABLE OF CONTENTS

Get to Know the Bears. 4

Bronko Nagurski 7

Mike Ditka 9

Gale Sayers 10

Dick Butkus 12

Walter Payton. 15

Brian Urlacher. 16

Kyle Long 19

Young Star 20

Team Fast Facts 22

Words to Know 23

Learn More 24

Index 24

GET TO KNOW THE BEARS

The Chicago Bears are the second oldest team in the NFL. Their **defense** is good. The Bears won a Super Bowl in 1985.

Who are some of the Bears' greatest stars? Let's find out!

BUSHROD
74
68

BRONKO NAGURSKI

Bronko Nagurski was one of the Bears' first stars. He was big and strong. He played **offense** and defense. He played in the NFL's first championship game in 1933. He even scored the winning touchdown for the Bears!

Ditka was the Bears' number one **draft** pick in 1961.

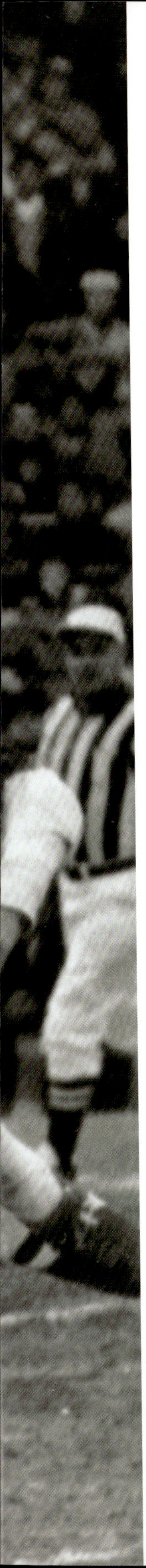

MIKE DITKA

Mike Ditka was a **tight end**. He was also good at catching passes. Ditka retired as a player in 1972. But he came back to coach the Bears in 1982. He led them to their Super Bowl win.

GALE SAYERS

Gale Sayers was fast. He was hard to catch. He scored six touchdowns in one game in 1965. He played in four **Pro Bowls**. He was named player of the game in three of them.

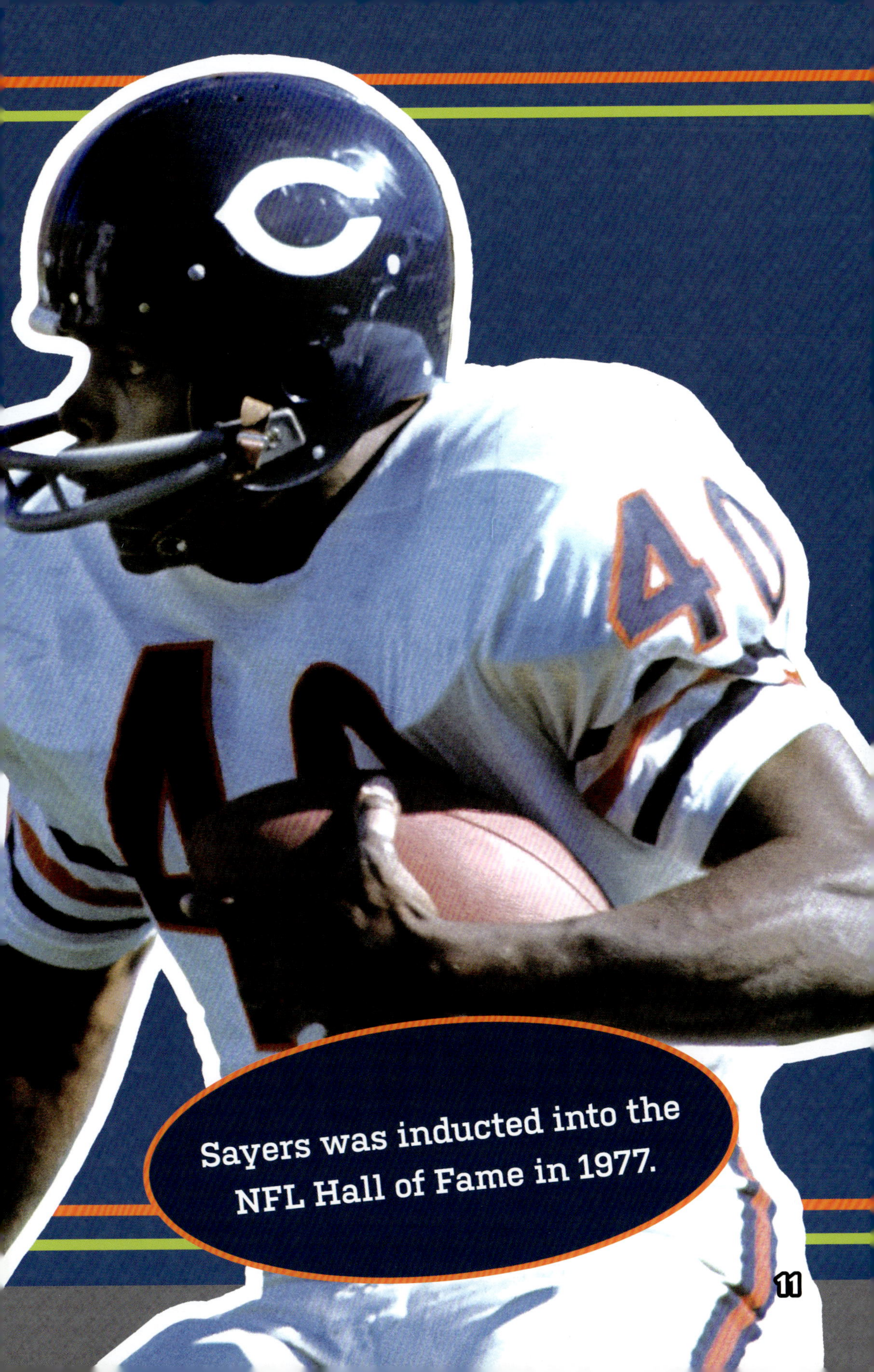

Sayers was inducted into the NFL Hall of Fame in 1977.

DICK BUTKUS

Some call Dick Butkus the best **linebacker** ever. He was smart. He was fast and strong, too. Few runners ever got past him. He retired in 1973.

It had been Butkus's dream to play pro football since the fifth grade.

WALTER PAYTON

Walter Payton was one of the best **running backs** of all time. He was fast on the field. Payton went to nine Pro Bowls. He was also named the 1977 **MVP** of the NFL.

BRIAN URLACHER

Brian Urlacher was a great tackler. He won an award for playing defense in 2005. He had 98 tackles. Urlacher has been to eight Pro Bowls. He retired in 2013. He played for the Bears for thirteen years.

Long played on the NFL's All-Rookie Team in 2013.

KYLE LONG

Kyle Long does a great job blocking. He joined the Bears in 2013. He has been to the Pro Bowl three times in a row. He played in his first Pro Bowl when he was just a **rookie**.

YOUNG STAR

Mitch Trubisky is a quarterback. The Bears picked him in the first round draft in 2017. He is fast. He has a good arm.

Let's watch and see who will be the next star of the Bears!

BEARS
GSH
Wilson

TEAM FAST FACTS

Founded: 1919

Nicknames: The Monsters of the Midway, Da Bears

Home Stadium: Soldier Field (Chicago, Illinois)

NFL Championships: 9 (1921, 1932, 1933, 1940, 1941, 1943, 1946, 1963, 1985)

Super Bowl Titles: 1 (1985)

Other Names: Decatur Staleys (1919-1920), Chicago Staleys (1921)

Hall of Fame Players: 34 including Bronko Nagurski, Mike Ditka, Gale Sayers, Dick Butkus, and Brian Urlacher

WORDS TO KNOW

defense – the group of players that tries to stop the other team from scoring

draft – an event where pro teams choose new players from college football teams

linebacker – a player whose main job is to tackle the other team's players so they cannot score

MVP – Most Valuable Player; an honor given to the best player each season

offense – the group of players that tries to score

Pro Bowl – the NFL's all-star game

rookie – a player in his first season

running back – a player whose main job is running with the ball

tight end – a player whose main jobs are to catch passes and block

LEARN MORE

Books

Burgess, Zach. *Meet the Chicago Bears*. Chicago: Norwood House Press, 2017.

Morey, Allan. *The Chicago Bears Story*. Minneapolis: Bellwether Media, Inc., 2017.

Websites

Chicago Bears—Official Site
http://www.chicagobears.com
Watch video clips and view photos of the Chicago Bears.

NFL Rush
http://www.nflrush.com
Play games and learn how to be a part of NFL PLAY 60.

NFL.com
http://nfl.com
Check out pictures and your favorite football players' stats.

Every effort has been made to ensure that these websites are appropriate for children. However, because of the nature of the Internet, it is impossible to guarantee that these sites will remain active indefinitely or that their contents will not be altered.

INDEX

All-Rookie Team, 18
Butkus, Dick, 12, 13
coach, 9
Ditka, Mike, 8, 9
Long, Kyle, 18, 19
MVP, 15
Nagurski, Bronko, 7
NFL, 4, 7, 11, 15, 18
NFL Hall of Fame, 11
Payton, Walter, 15
Pro Bowl, 10, 15, 16, 19
retire, 9, 12, 16
Sayers, Gale, 10, 11
Super Bowl, 4, 9
Trubisky, Mitch, 20
Urlacher, Brian, 16